Original title:
Sunlit Spaces

Copyright © 2025 Creative Arts Management OÜ
All rights reserved.

Author: Finn Donovan
ISBN HARDBACK: 978-1-80581-786-4
ISBN PAPERBACK: 978-1-80581-313-2
ISBN EBOOK: 978-1-80581-786-4

A Symphony of Sunbeams

A cat on a windowsill, oh what a sight,
Basking in brilliance, chasing dust in flight.
The dog chews a sock, with glee it runs,
While sunspots dance for all the silly ones.

The flowers rise up, with faces aglow,
Laughing at shadows that duck for a show.
Pigeons play tag with the breeze on the run,
And ants hold auditions, a march for the fun!

Embracing the Golden Hours

A toddler laughs, with cake on its face,
While butterflies flutter, they pick up the pace.
Squirrels debate who can climb the best tree,
In a world full of mischief, so playful and free.

The picnic is wild, with sandwiches tossed,
Someone yells, 'Hey, I think something's lost!'
A frisbee flies high, but lands on a hat,
Who knew sun-kissed moments could lead to such chat?

Luminous Lullabies

The lamp on the table hums a soft tune,
Matched only by giggles that float like a balloon.
Fairy lights twinkle through a dance with the night,
As shadows go waltzing, a whimsical sight.

In this merry land where the laughter persists,
A gnome plays chess with a squirrel who twists.
They argue for hours, each puffing their cheeks,
While the cosmos winks, simply loving the freaks.

Cheerful Corners in Between

Over in the corner, the plants have a chat,
One claims to be grandpa, though he's really a sprat.
The curtains are swinging, in joy they sway,
As sunlight tickles and whispers, 'Let's play!'

A couch cushions grumble, they yell with delight,
Daring the dust bunnies to join for a fight.
With cushions in clouds and laughter galore,
Life's a mad tea party—who could ask for more?

Radiance in the Quiet Nook

There's a spot where shadows play,
A mouse once thought it was his stay.
I offered him a cup of tea,
He laughed and ran, 'Not for me!'

A cat snuck in to steal my chair,
She yawned at sunlight's gentle flair.
I tried to shoo her out with glee,
She purred and said, 'It's cozy, see?'

Dappled Dreams of Daylight

In the morning light, so bright and clear,
I chased a butterfly, oh dear!
It danced away, what a clever trick,
I tripped and fell—my legs went slick!

The flowers giggled, 'Catch us too!'
I spun around, 'What else to do?'
They swayed and twirled in a silly line,
I joined the waltz, feeling just fine.

Whispers of Warmth Through the Leaves

A squirrel pondered on a branch,
In the sun, he took a chance.
He slipped and tumbled, made a dash,
The ground was soft, it was quite a crash!

His friends all laughed, 'What a show!'
He shook his fur, 'I'm just a pro!'
With a flip and flop, he claimed his prize,
A nut, while groans mixed with the cries.

Glimmers between the Shadows

A light bulb flickered, buzzed with pride,
It dreamt of disco, oh what a ride!
The bugs all gathered, ready to groove,
But got too close, it made them move!

They did the cha-cha on the floor,
A hum of laughter, oh what a score!
The shadows joined in, quite absurd,
A dance-off ruled by a quirky bird!

A Canvas of Golden Light

In the park, I see a flake,
That's not a bird! It's a cake.
A squirrel steals it, looking spry,
As frosting flies up to the sky.

An artist trails with his big brush,
Painting flowers in a rush.
But bees think he's a big ol' snack,
They buzz around him—what a hack!

Chasing Light in the Garden

I ran to catch that glow so bright,
Tripped on a gnome—what a fright!
The flowers giggle in delight,
As I roll past, a funny sight.

The ladybugs plot with a grin,
As I chase shadows round and round.
They take to the air, such a spin,
And I just laugh, I'm off the ground!

Where Brightness Meets the Breeze

The wind whispers secrets so sweet,
It tickles the grass beneath my feet.
I dance with daffodils in my hand,
While worms sing songs, a quirky band.

A butterfly lands on my nose,
It seems to giggle, she knows how it goes.
We laugh at a cat, all curled in a ball,
As a leaf falls down, we have a ball!

Luminous Echoes of Afternoon

The sun spills gold on the playground swings,
Where laughter's the tune all the fun brings.
A kid flies high, nearly hits the moon,
While parents sip drinks, toasting with a tune.

A dog chases shadows, what a silly race,
He trips on his tail—oh, what a face!
The day ends with fireflies—small winks of light,
And the world wraps us in joy, oh so bright!

Elysium of Enchanted Glows

In meadows where the bees take naps,
A snail in shades just maps its laps.
A bright-eyed bunny hops with flair,
While daisies giggle, unaware.

The sun dresses trees in golden cheer,
Squirrels in bow ties swing near.
Butterflies host a dance-off spree,
As ants just wonder, 'Where's my tea?'

A wise old turtle smirks with glee,
Saying, "Life's a race, but not for me!"
Chasing shadows, a cat makes a leap,
And stumbles into a fragrant heap.

With each mad chase, the laughter grows,
As sunlight drips on furry toes.
In this enchanted, vibrant frame,
Every creature knows the game!

Serenity Awash in Warm Tones

In gardens where the laughter floats,
The worms wear hats and tell strange jokes.
A bobbing duck quacks on cue,
While flowers bloom in shades of blue.

The butterflies wear shades of bright,
While grasshoppers groove in the light.
A frog croaks out a wicked pun,
As daisies nod, just having fun.

Bumblebees with bling on wings,
Buzzing tales of springtime flings.
A ladybug spins round and round,
While butterflies form a conga sound.

Amidst this cheer, a squirrel flips,
Over nuts and fuzzy quips.
Together here, life's laughter stirs,
In the warmth, we chase our furs!

Nature's Whispered Revelations

In forests where the sunlight beams,
A raccoon reads his comic dreams.
The pines lean in to hear the joke,
While laughing streams dance as they croak.

A chipmunk's stash of acorns grows,
He hides them well, or so he knows.
With every nibble, he makes sure,
His secrets stay a cheerful blur.

A wily fox plays hide and seek,
With grouchy owls who can't speak.
He's dressed in leaves and fragile twigs,
While crickets hum their funky gigs.

As shadows stretch and day drifts low,
The laughter echoes, soft and slow.
Together here, the wild things play,
In whispered glee till end of day!

Daydreams on Radiant Trails

In bright fields where the grass may tickle,
I chase butterflies, and I laugh, oh what a fickle!
They tease me with their flutters in the air,
While I tumble and twist with my messy hair.

A chipmunk mocks me, with a tiny little laugh,
As I trip over daisies, what a silly gaffe!
Yet as I roll, I spot a cloud-shaped pie,
I wish upon it—oh, let this slice be nigh!

The Magic of Early Light

The rooster crows, but I'm not awake yet,
Decorating dreams with bright ribbons, what a set!
I blame the bedsheets; they're too cozy for me,
Each strand like a spell, casting sweet, lazy glee.

Coffee spills, a morning disaster, quite grand,
While I do the morning dance—cup in hand!
But those golden rays sneak in, a playful tease,
Maybe today I'll finally dance with the breeze!

Shimmering Spaces of Solitude

In my secret lair, where mischief brews,
I find odd socks that I'm supposed to choose.
With crayons and doodles all over my face,
Turns out my art's just a wild, messy place.

The cat's my critic, judging my flair,
She rolls her eyes, as if she truly cares.
Yet amidst the chaos, laughter rises high,
In this glittering bubble, oh how dreams fly!

Nature's Gentle Brushstrokes

A squirrel with style steals my last french fry,
He twirls and he prances, oh look at him fly!
While flowers gossip in whispers so sweet,
The bees have joined in for a dance to repeat.

I nod with a grin at the blossoms' bright show,
While ants march proudly in a row, row, row.
In this bustling chaos, I find my delight,
Nature's a jester, bringing joy to my sight!

Soft Hush of Light

In a room where shadows play,
A cat dances, dreaming away.
She pounces on beams, all a-glow,
Chasing dust flecks, stealing the show.

The curtains flutter, oh what a tease,
A reluctant laugh from the old oak trees.
As whispers of warmth tickle the air,
Socks off, my feet find the chill—do I care?

Revelations of the Rising Sun

At dawn, I trip over my shoes,
A rooster sings; I start to snooze!
Coffee's brewing, spilling a lot,
Why can't I be like my coffee pot?

The toast pops up, a quick salute,
It lands face-down, what a hoot!
Pancakes flip like they've got plans,
While I argue with my drying hands.

Evocations of Golden Hours

In the garden, weeds play hide and seek,
While squirrels mock me with a loud cheek.
The daisies laugh as I stumble near,
I swear they are jesters in flowered gear!

Butterflies hover, making a show,
While I try to shoo off the bees, oh no!
An ants' parade, marching my way,
Guess I'll join them—who wants to play?

Sun-kissed Secrets of the Earth

Under the tree, a picnic unfolds,
Leftover snacks, or so I was told.
But a squirrel claims my last cookie,
I guess I'll settle for some green mookie!

The grass tickles—oh, seize the fun!
A dance-off with bugs? Now I'm done!
Sharing secrets with ants on the ground,
Who knew such humor could abound?

Sparkling Secrets of the Clearing

In a clearing, squirrels leap,
Whispers small, they love to peep.
A dance of shadows, flick and flit,
Who knew nuts were such a hit?

Mice hold parties, cheese galore,
Tiny feet tap on the floor.
A rabbit serves the finest tea,
Toads applaud, "Oh, what glee!"

Branches clap, what a delight,
As fireflies twinkle through the night.
Nature's jesters, full of cheer,
In the clearing, all's a sphere.

So if you wander, take a look,
Secrets hide in every nook.
Just beware of playful pranks,
For in this place, we free our banks!

Light's Serenade Amongst the Flora

Bumblebees hum a lovely tune,
While flowers sway, like kids in June.
They giggle when a breeze does blow,
Tickling petals, putting on a show.

Sunbeams tap-dance on bright leaves,
A chorus of cheer in nature's cleaves.
Daffodils wear their fancy hats,
As butterflies join in with chats.

Beetles boast of their fine rides,
As ladybugs take joyful strides.
In this realm where colors play,
Every moment's bright and gay.

So grab a seat on mossy stones,
Listen close for nature's groans.
For when the light reveals the jest,
Among the flora, life is best!

Tapestry of Brightness in Bloom

Petals flutter, a dazzling sight,
Colors burst, bringing pure delight.
A tapestry woven with laughter and cheer,
With hidden jokes, that all come here.

Daisies whisper to the bumblebee,
"Join our game, come count with me."
While tulips giggle, swaying in glee,
Rabbits chuckle, "What frolics we see!"

Violets play hide and seek with the breeze,
A game of sneak that's sure to please.
Carnations twirl, perform and sway,
In this bright bloom, we'll laugh all day.

So join the fun, let worries fade,
In this garden, jokes are laid.
A tapestry of smiles and light,
In every bloom, pure, silly delight!

Resplendent Paths Through the Woods

In the woods, where shadows play,
Every corner hides a display.
A squirrel dressed in tiny shoes,
Singing songs of morning blues.

Mushrooms step to an unseen beat,
Crickets chirp, oh what a feat!
A raccoon's got a grand parade,
Their float made from a fallen spade.

Stumps hold meetings, squirrels debate,
What's the best way to celebrate?
Berries giggle, ripe and sweet,
Telling tales to all they meet.

So take a stroll, let laughter soar,
In these paths, find glee galore.
For every tree has laughs to lend,
In the woods, joys never end!

The Alchemy of Daylight

In the morning light, I dance around,
Stumbling on shadows that fall to the ground.
Giggling at birds that steal my toast,
Fleeting little thieves, they're the breakfast host.

The sun spills gold on my morning brew,
Turns my sleepy frown into a sunlit view.
I tip my hat to the clouds, so fluffy,
As they remind me: my hair looks puffy!

Laughter erupts like bubbles in air,
Chasing after butterflies without a care.
The day's bright laughter, contagious and loud,
Draws a giggly crowd beneath the soft cloud.

Chasing sunbeams instead of my dreams,
Finding joy in the silliest schemes.
The magic of light tosses worries away,
As I revel in fun throughout the day.

Paths of Illumination

Wandering paths where the daisies play,
I trip on a rock that's rolled in my way.
Giggling flowers wagging their heads,
While I'm serenaded by whispers of threads.

The hedges giggle, the trees all grin,
As squirrels stage a race, watch them begin.
Joyful pursuits under the bright sheen,
Where every corner hides a new scene.

Sunbeams tickle the tips of my nose,
A warm, silly tickle that playfully knows.
I dance with shadows, they twirl right back,
Creating a melody, a silly knack.

Paths of laughter twine here and there,
Each step brings forth a comedic flare.
Nature's own stage, the best of the lot,
A funny performance, I've got the spot.

Twilight's Gentle Surrender

As daylight fades, the shadows expand,
I wrestle with fireflies, they laugh at my hand.
Their flickering lights, such a playful tease,
Like tiny warm giggles spun in the breeze.

The sun whispers secrets while fading away,
I hold onto shadows that want to stay.
Chasing the twilight, I trip on my feet,
Stumbling on dreams that feel oh-so-sweet.

The moon rolls in with a chuckle and grin,
He knows all my secrets and spins in a spin.
What a funny world, this dance of the night,
As I tip my hat to the fading sunlight.

A joking farewell from the day so bright,
With twinkling stars to guide me at night.
Twilight whispers, "Don't take it too serious,"
In playful abandon, the dark can be curious.

Basking in Nature's Glow

I sprawl on the grass, my crown made of leaves,
Counting the clouds, they're like fluffy thieves.
Each one whispers jokes that make my heart beam,
While I sip on the nectar of a wildflower dream.

The sun giggles softly, a tickling breeze,
Teasing my hair, like it aims to please.
Butterflies flutter, it's a colorful show,
As I bask in this glow, my heart starts to flow.

A squirrel does ballet, a real funny sight,
While I chuckle softly, basking in light.
Nature's own stage with a whimsical air,
Every leaf and twig sings, "Join us, if you dare!"

The laughter around me dances and sways,
In this snickering symphony, I start my plays.
Basking in moments that shine and ignite,
I find my own path in this comic delight.

The Dance of Light and Leaf

In the park, the shadows play,
Leaves jiggle in a merry sway.
A squirrel dips, a bird will prance,
While sunlight gives the trees a chance.

The grass giggles, tickled bright,
Chasing shadows, oh what a sight!
Gnarled roots join the frolic cheer,
As the sun throws its laughter near.

Hopping stones, a gleeful game,
The friendly breeze will share the fame.
Watch how petals dance and swirl,
In this sunlight-filled, leafy whirl.

Nature's jest, a playful tease,
Whispers humor through the trees.
With every ray and each warm beam,
Life's a conga line, it seems!

Embracing the Glow of Serenity

A lazy bee buzzes with glee,
While flowers hum their harmony.
The daisies lounge, soak up the rays,
In radiant light, they softly sway.

A chubby caterpillar grins,
Knowing soon, a dance begins.
Underneath, the daisies laugh,
In their petals, a cunning craft.

The sunshine spills like honey, sweet,
While ants waltz on tiny feet.
With sunlight warm, they dream and shout,
A fairytale's what life's about!

Grasshoppers leap and start to sing,
What joy the golden days will bring!
In this glow, hearts come alive,
As laughter blooms, we all survive!

Rays Caressing the Mossy Floor

Morning light, a silly tease,
Kisses moss with joyful ease.
Tadpoles splash, in quirk so grand,
With sunlight's wink, they take a stand.

Mossy carpets hold secrets tight,
While bugs spin tales in pure delight.
Crickets chirp in harmony,
As nature writes its symphony.

A wiggly worm with stories rife,
Offers up his sunny life.
Underneath a leafy dome,
The critters know they're never alone.

With golden rays that giggle low,
They weave through tall grass in a flow.
Joining in this frolicking score,
Life's a party, oh, what a chore!

A Moment of Joy in the Brightness

Here comes the sun with laughter loud,
Tickling flowers, drawing a crowd.
Puddles splash with every leap,
As sunlight cradles earth in sleep.

The bunnies binkie, oh what grace!
With floppy ears, they roam and race.
Butterflies join the parade of cheer,
Whirling colors that disappear.

The bees, they wear a golden smile,
While ants march in a bold file.
Each ray bounces, a gleeful burst,
In this delight, we all must thirst.

So catch a beam, and share it wide,
In this glow, let fun abide.
With every giggle in the breeze,
Joy ignites the hearts with ease!

In the Heart of a Meadow

In fields where daisies wear their hats,
A rabbit danced with chubby rats.
They chewed on grass and made a cheer,
Declaring how the snacks were near.

The butterflies took to the air,
With wobbly grace, they had no care.
A bumblebee tried to join the show,
But tripped on petals—oh, oh, no!

A squirrel perched on a throne of leaves,
Announced, 'It's time for our reprieves!'
The piñata made of clover blooms,
Broke open to release plump plumes.

And as the shadows danced about,
A frog just leapt—a joyful shout!
In this odd realm where mischief plays,
We laughed away the sunny days.

Glistening Pathways

Along the path where sparkles gleam,
A snail was caught—his slow-paced dream.
He waved at ants racing round and loud,
'Watch me zoom!' he said, feeling proud.

A lizard wore a tiny cap,
Said, 'Time for sun! Let's take a nap!'
But then a breeze, so bold and sly,
Flipped his hat into the sky!

Mice threw shade from shady spots,
As squirrels stole their lunch in knots.
And as they chased with squeaks and glee,
They bumped a hedgehog—oh, dear me!

Yet on this road of laughter sweet,
Every creature found a treat.
With giggles high and troubles low,
The glistening path began to glow.

Glows of Tranquility

In a corner where calm winds play,
A cat reclined, dreaming away.
He whispered secrets to a stone,
'Life's just fine when you're alone!'

The goldfish splashed with wild delight,
Had grand dreams of a dance tonight.
They organized a splashy crew,
And practiced moves that none could do.

A frog composed a serenade,
To serenade a passing parade.
With croaks and bubbles, quite the sound,
'Frogstar' badges soon were crowned!

As night fell softly with a sigh,
Stars blinked down from the velvet sky.
In this peaceful place of fun and cheer,
Laughter echoed without a fear.

Dappled Dreams of Dawn

At dawn, where beams of laughter shine,
A crow wore shades, proclaimed, 'I'm fine!'
The morning dew, in sparkles bright,
   Made rabbits hop with pure delight.

The flowers yawned, began to stretch,
While beetles played a game to fetch.
With laughter pure, they rolled and pranced,
   Inviting all to join the dance.

A sleepy owl blinked and grinned,
'Good morning, friends! Let's begin!'
A parade of critters, bright and bold,
   Strolled through stories yet untold.

As sunlight painted shades of cheer,
All creatures knew that fun was near.
In joy-filled meadows, come what may,
The dawn would bring a brand-new play.

A Canvas of Warm Hues

In a world where shadows leap,
Painted smiles, they never sleep.
Ducks in hats, they waddle by,
While giggles float up to the sky.

A patch of grass, so bright and green,
Where ants wear shades, it's quite the scene.
Squirrels dance in a conga line,
With acorns as their mighty wine.

The sun tickles the blooming flowers,
They laugh at all their growing hours.
Jellybeans rain down from above,
A sugary feast we all can love!

Painting life with hues so bold,
Every moment, a story told.
His jokes are corny, but that's okay,
We all laugh and dance, come what may.

The Charm of Brighter Hours

The morning sun, a playful face,
Turns sleepy heads into a race.
Cats sport ties, in a boardroom scene,
Purring profits, nothing so keen!

Birds with top hats sing a tune,
Exchanging gossip with the moon.
They chirp of clouds that stole their pie,
While the sun chuckles in the sky.

The grass tickles toes, it's a prank,
As ants march in their perfect rank.
Toys come alive when the light is bright,
Building castles until the night.

Joy spills over, a golden spill,
On lemonade laughs that give a thrill.
With friends like these, we dance and shout,
In brightened hours, we laugh it out!

Hues of Happiness

In fields of joy, we bounce around,
Clowns on stilts, we all astound.
Bubbles float like dreams in air,
While giggles sparkle everywhere.

A pumpkin rides a skateboard fast,
With silly faces, we all laugh past.
The rhythm of daisies shakes the ground,
As butterflies twirl, they spin around.

Under trees with candy leaves,
Lollipops grow, oh what a tease!
Cookie crumbs scatter as we dash,
To catch the rainbow's playful splash.

With every hue, our laughter swells,
In a world where joy compels.
Let's paint our day and never stop,
In our garden of giggles, let's hop!

Elysian Rays in Hidden Nooks

In cozy corners, smiles ignite,
With cups of cocoa, all feels right.
A hedgehog wears a tiny hat,
As he argues with a snoozing cat.

The rays sneak in, a golden crew,
Throwing sparkles on the dew.
Giggling flowers, they sway their heads,
While frogs discuss their bedtime beds.

The secret paths where laughter blooms,
Shine like the brightest summer rooms.
With silly jokes and ticklish grass,
We share our joys, let time just pass.

In hidden nooks, where echoes play,
We dance until the end of day.
Where sunlight brightens every face,
Creating joy in every space.

Where Happiness Meets the Sky

In a field where laughter plays,
And sunshine dances in a daze.
The cows wear hats, the sheep can sing,
While roosters boast of everything.

Frogs wear ties to croak their bets,
And squirrels share their nutty threats.
With every step, a giggle springs,
As butterflies perform their flings.

A rabbit juggles carrots round,
While ants parade without a sound.
The breezy whispers tell a tale,
Where joy and nonsense never pale.

So come and join this silly spree,
Where happiness is wild and free.
A world where whimsy holds the key,
To the best kind of hilarity!

Echoes of a Honeyed Glow

In golden rays the bees do buzz,
While flowers giggle, just because.
The breeze plays tricks, it tugs your shirt,
As daisies tease, they cause a flirt.

A cat wears shades and strikes a pose,
While chubby clouds do funny shows.
Each shadow prances, winks, and sways,
As sunlight teases through the haze.

The ants have formed a marching band,
With tiny trumpets at demand.
They march in time, all in a line,
Disguised as toast, they're feeling fine.

So laugh along with nature's song,
Where every critter plays along.
In this sweet glow, let's giggle more,
As echoes of joy dance on the floor!

Chambers of Captivating Light

In a room where shadows are quite shy,
A hamster hosts a tea party high.
With tiny cups and crumpets laid,
The laughter spills, it won't cascade.

The lamp has legs, it does a jig,
And chairs take turns to dance a gig.
While curtains sway in playful glee,
As sunlight bursts in fiery spree.

There's mischief in the glittering beams,
As cups hold secrets, whispered dreams.
A calendar laughs at silly dates,
With doodles of cats that contemplate.

So join the fun in this grand space,
Where every corner holds a face.
Each beam a jest, each shadow bright,
In chambers filled with pure delight!

The Essence of a Bright Day

When morning breaks with giggles near,
And toast pops high with misspelled cheer.
A blender sings its silly tune,
As waffles dance beneath the moon.

The flowers wear their brightest hats,
While playful kittens chase their sprats.
A bird in shades sings out of key,
Creating chaos, wild and free.

Picnics filled with treats that bounce,
As ants parade and all take pounce.
The sunlight sparkles on the dew,
While everything seems fresh and new.

Let's bask in joy, come what may,
Each moment's bright in its own way.
With laughter painting life's display,
We revel in this funny play!

Fluttering Moments in Sunbeam Halls

In rooms where shadows tap their toes,
The dust bunnies dance, striking poses.
Chasing sunbeams, they skate on floors,
While giggling curtains peek through doors.

A cat in a bowtie, oh what a sight,
He waltzes with mice, oh what a fright!
But they laugh and twirl, no spirit to fret,
In sunlight's embrace, no room for regret.

A dog with a hat, lost in his chase,
Tripping on feet, it's a comical race.
They cartwheel through laughter, a sky of delight,
Like cookies on trays in a whimsical flight.

With giggles and chuckles, the hours just flit,
In rooms warmed by joy, where every soul fits.
So join in the frolic and feel the warmth rise,
In the fluttering moments, let spirit surprise.

Skylight Lullabies in the Meadow

In fields where daisies softly sway,
The rabbits hum tunes, come out to play.
As butterflies giggle, they tickle the air,
With a hop and a bounce, joy is everywhere.

A hedgehog on stilts has a talent so neat,
While grasshoppers sing in a rhythmic beat.
Unicorns prance with invisible flair,
Under the blue, they dance without care.

The sunbeams sprinkle laughter, full of cheer,
As nutty young squirrels bring everyone near.
With acorns in pockets, they plot and they scheme,
Using shadows as canvases, painting their dream.

When twilight's drawing, they gather around,
Sharing their stories, no secrets unbound.
In the meadow of giggles, the night sings delight,
Where skylight lullabies make everything right.

Golden Glimmers of Hope

In kitchens where cookies demand to be seen,
The mess turns to laughter, a baker's routine.
With splats and with drips, oh what a delight,
As the clock ticks time, the frosting takes flight.

A parrot named Gregory sings tunes out of key,
While stealing the bread, a true jubilee.
With feathers so bright and mischief so bold,
He shares the sweet chaos that never gets old.

The old hound takes naps, snoring loud as a drum,
While kids plan a heist for the last piece of gum.
Together they giggle, their joy never fades,
Creating those moments that sunlight pervades.

With golden glimmers, the laughter is shared,
In a world full of warmth, love is declared.
So munch on those snacks, let your worries elope,
For joy in small bites is our grandest hope.

Radiance in the Quiet Corner

In nooks where the cushions are plush and so grand,
A bear with a book has a quite silly plan.
He sips on some tea, from a tiny red cup,
And giggles at squirrels who just won't give up.

A snail wearing glasses, so wise and so slow,
Gives life lessons wrapped in a slow-moving flow.
With a wink and a nod, he grants them a peek,
That wisdom needs time and a sprinkle of freak.

As sunlight cascades into corners of cheer,
The shadows keep dancing, not feeling the fear.
A ladybug lounges, sipping on dew,
Sharing tales of adventures, both funny and true.

So cuddle those cushions, let laughter unfold,
In corners of quiet, bright stories are told.
Where smiles are contagious, and warmth fills the air,
In the radiance found, we find what we share.

Cherished Escapes Beneath Bright Skies

In a park where frogs play chess,
The ducks judge them, what a mess!
Kids giggle as ants march in line,
While I wonder if squirrels drink wine.

Kites fly high, like dreams set free,
But one gets stuck—oh, woe is me!
The wind laughs loud, a mischievous friend,
As I chase my kite—it just won't bend.

Picnics turn into feasts of ants,
My sandwich now part of their dance.
Laughter echoes off the trees,
As we all toast with wasp-sweet teas.

Beneath the sun's cheeky, warm glow,
We dance around like in a show.
With joy filling up every nook,
In this bright world, just take a look!

The Lure of a Bright Horizon

A lemonade stand on a bumpy road,
The sign's so crooked, it's a new code!
Kids sell dreams with giggles and grins,
While I sip lemonade, where's my gin?

Bicycles race, wheels flying quick,
One rider's pants split—what a trick!
Laughter erupts like a fizzy pop,
As we watch him scream and hopefully stop.

The horizon winks with a playful gleam,
Clouds do the cha-cha, or so it seems.
Sunshine tickles the daisies bright,
Nature's silly, but feels so right.

Chasing shadows, we run and leap,
Stumbling over paths, both wide and steep.
With every laugh and silly fall,
We find ourselves 'neath the sky's great hall.

Hills of Light and Laughter

Rolling hills where giggles flow,
We tumble down, just like a show.
My friend yells "Stop!" but I'm in flight,
I trip on laughter, what a sight!

Picnic blankets full of fluff,
But ants bring snacks; it's just too tough.
We try to eat while bats do dive,
Hot dogs fly—it's a food fight hive!

Kites chase clouds in silly loops,
While squirrels mock us, forming troops.
I throw a frisbee, it twirls and bends,
Nabbing my shoe—sorry, right to the ends!

With every tumble down this hill,
Laughter bounces, it's quite the thrill.
Amidst it all, we know for sure,
These hills keep us coming back for more!

Sanctuaries of Warm Radiance

Under trees where shadows dance,
We find a world that loves the chance.
Butterflies wear hats that are absurd,
In this warm glow, nothing's unheard.

The sun throws tantrums—what a scene,
In puddles, we splash like we're all keen.
Laughter sparkles in every ray,
Guess who fell in? She'll be okay!

Pine cones tickle as we race,
A dusty trail's our happy place.
We tuck our worries in puffy clouds,
Chasing light, laughing out loud.

With cookies stolen from mom's stash,
We feast like kings, loud and brash.
In this oasis, so bright and fair,
Each chuckle becomes a sunbeam's flare!

Whispered Glow in the Garden

In the garden, a snail wears a hat,
Bouncing along, just a tip of the spat.
Flowers giggle, not afraid to say,
"Look at that guy, what a silly display!"

Bees buzz around, in a dance that's loud,
While the cat pretends to be part of the crowd.
A frog croaks jokes on his lily pad throne,
His punchlines land like well-thrown stones!

Ladybugs chuckle as they take their flight,
Holding a party, oh what a sight!
With each little flicker, the fireflies show,
The laughter that blossoms, more sweet than a flow.

So come join the fun, in this patch of delight,
Where creatures convene and all hearts feel light.
In whispered tones, the garden will sing,
"Let's laugh till the stars come and dance in the spring!"

Where Shadows Yield to Brightness

In the park where the shadows play tag,
A squirrel steals snacks while wearing a rag.
The sun pops out, chasing clouds like a game,
As children giggle, they call out his name!

A dog wearing glasses is chasing his tail,
While butterflies flutter, avoiding the pale.
A picnic is spread, with sandwiches stacked,
Then ants stage a heist – what a bold act!

Kites dance above in a colorful race,
While a rogue balloon floats, it's lost in the grace.
Each moment a picture, such joy on display,
Even shadows are smiling, they know how to play!

When day fades to dusk, and laughter is deep,
The echoes of joy will forever keep.
In the park where the light and the shadows unite,
Funny tales blossom – oh what a delight!

Illuminated Moments

In the kitchen, the toaster pops bread with a cheer,
While the cat contemplates culinary fear.
A spatula dances, flipping pancakes with flair,
As everyone giggles – who'll throw flour in the air?

The sun peeks in with a mischievous grin,
And the fridge hums tunes as the chaos begins.
Garlic smells sweet as the chef takes a whirl,
But oops! He spills sauce, look at that swirl!

The clock ticks in rhythm, with a jolly old song,
While goofy faces try to get along.
Each moment's a treasure, so funny and bright,
As laughter erupts in the morning light.

So remember these times, filled with joy and glee,
In these whimsical moments, set your heart free.
Let kitchen adventures be forever so grand,
With giggles and grins always close at hand!

The Laughter of Daylight

In the morning, a rooster crows with a wink,
While the dogs all bark as they plot and think.
A parade of shadows struts across the road,
Bouncing with laughter, all lighthearted and bold!

Grasshoppers leap, telling puns to the breeze,
While the daisies snicker and sway with ease.
The sun serves up warmth like pancakes on plates,
As laughter erupts from mysterious crates!

With every bright ray, a giggle expands,
Even the trees are waving their hands.
The rhythm of nature, a comical tune,
As ants march in lines, all in pursuit of a boon!

So join in the chorus, let laughter run free,
In the daylight's embrace, there's no need to flee.
With the world so alive in this whimsical quest,
Let the jokes of the morning become your new best!

Illuminating Winks of Life

A squirrel in shades, what a sight,
Winking at me in morning light.
He's got a secret, it seems quite grand,
Nutty plans crafted by furry hand.

A cat in a sunbeam, oh so sly,
Pretending to chase as the birds fly high.
She rolls and she stretches, it's quite absurd,
Claiming the kingdom without a word.

The flowers giggle in their vibrant hues,
Telling each other their daily news.
With buzzing bees in a dance so neat,
They plot and they scheme, all while they eat.

A kite takes off, but not quite right,
Diving for grass, what a comical flight!
With laughter and joy in the open breeze,
Life's silly moments, a perfect tease.

A Glimpse of Warmth in the Wilderness

A deer tripped over a twig, what a show,
Covered in leaves, trying to go slow.
He shook it off with a dramatic flair,
That mischievous look on his face laid bare.

A bear in a hammock, swaying along,
Singing a tune, oh, what a song!
He's sipping honey from a little cup,
Ambassadors of fun, he's living it up.

The sun peeks through, all giggles and beams,
As critters embark on their funny dreams.
A raccoon juggles acorns with glee,
Sparks of laughter float through the trees.

Down by the river, the fish seem to play,
Jumping and splashing in a breezy ballet.
With each silly leap, they flick and they flap,
Nature's best jester, what a raucous clap!

The Touch of Day and Night

When day takes a break in the play of the dusk,
The moon winks at stars, it's surely a must.
The crickets start tuning their evening song,
Their chorus of chirps seems lively and strong.

A raccoon dons shades as the sun drops low,
Sipping his drink while putting on a show.
He raises his paw, giving us a wink,
Evening antics, oh, what a link!

Fireflies twinkle in a playful dance,
Flirting with shadows, given a chance.
They dodge and they dart, the night their throne,
Giggling softly, never alone.

As night stretches out, a cuddly bear yawns,
Dreaming of honey till the fresh dawn.
In this playful world, so bright and so spry,
Day and night get together to fly!

Glimmers in the Stillness

Sitting by the pond, frogs start their chat,
Ribbiting tales in a splashy spat.
Each jump is a laugh, a comedic spree,
With lily pads serving as seats for the tea.

A turtle takes selfies, oh what a treat,
Posing just right with a twig for his feet.
He smiles wide, as if to say,
'Life's about laughter, come join my way!'

In the quiet of twilight, the owls convene,
Sharing their shenanigans, a sight so serene.
With hoots of friendship echoing clear,
Together they laugh without any fear.

The gentle breeze carries stories untold,
Whispering secrets through the branches so bold.
In these moments of peace, while giggles resound,
Nature's humor brings joy all around.

Effervescent Breezes and Golden Leaves

The trees wear hats made of yellow and red,
While squirrels engage in a disco instead.
With giggles and guffaws, the critters play,
As leaves jump around, they join the ballet.

The wind whispers jokes that tickle the air,
While acorns chuckle without a care.
Frolicking shadows dance on the ground,
In this playful realm, hilarity's found.

Bubbles of laughter, they float all around,
In this whimsical world, joy can be found.
The sun winks down, adding cheer to the day,
As we join the fun, come what may!

With every gust, a feathered friend sings,
A chorus of chuckles from all kinds of things.
Effervescent breezes, a jovial spree,
In the land of the wacky, we sip our tea!

Mosaic of Nature's Palette

Paint splatters of green, orange, and gold,
Nature's own canvas, a sight to behold.
A rabbit in spectacles, a real sight to see,
Critiquing the colors, as bold as can be!

With a brush and a wink, the flowers resound,
As butterflies giggle and prance all around.
Each petal a note in a symphonic tune,
As the daisies debate who's best in the bloom!

A maze of wild hues from violet to rose,
The bees wear tuxedos, who knows how it goes?
While ants steal the show, in their marching parade,
Creating a spectacle that simply won't fade.

Who knew that each color could bring such delight,
In this quirky escapade, everything's light!
So pop a confetti, let laughter ignite,
In this mosaic of joy, let's dance through the night!

Twinkling Trails of Bliss

The path is alive with giggles and cheer,
As mushrooms wear hats and say "Hi there, dear!"
With stardust in pockets, they twinkle and jive,
These trails full of whimsy are truly alive!

Each step is a spark in this vibrant game,
While critters make puns that will never feel lame.
Fireflies play tag in the shimmering dark,
With laughter so bright, it ignites a spark!

Dandelions flash smiles with fluffy white puffs,
While rabbits in bowties declare that it's tough.
To keep up with this riot of rollicking fun,
As shadows do somersaults under the sun!

So venture down paths where giggles abound,
And let every twinkle bring joy all around.
On these trails of delightful, let worries dismiss,
Join the frolicsome procession of bliss!

Luminosity in Hidden Paths

In secretive lanes where the chuckles persist,
Glow-worms tell tales with a twist of their wrist.
With giggles all around, the trees eavesdrop,
While mushrooms breakdance, they never will stop!

The hedgehogs are in capes; they claim it's their night,
As crickets throw shadows in a comic delight.
With every soft rustle, a punchline is found,
As the forest erupts with whimsical sound!

Among the tall ferns, the laughter might bloom,
In this realm of mischief, there's never a gloom.
Colorful lanterns dance in the breeze,
As the moon cracks a joke, it's a comedic tease!

So stroll through these alleys where magic's in sight,
With luminescent laughter that's pure and so light.
On hidden paths, let your troubles erase,
In the glow of this joy, find your funny place!

Daydreams Under Cloudless Blues

Balloons float high, a silent race,
Chasing the clouds, they find their place.
Giggling flowers in vibrant bloom,
Swapping jokes with the buzzing broom.

A squirrel in shades, sipping lime,
Critiques the mailman, oh what a crime!
Kites dance freely, all in a twirl,
While ants throw a party, watch 'em whirl!

Rum-tum-tiddle on the grass so green,
Worms draw mustaches, it's quite the scene.
Each breeze whispers secrets, oh so sweet,
Our laughter echoes, can't accept defeat!

With lemonade wishes, we're sailing along,
In this bright world, life sings a song.
So here's to daydreams, wild and carefree,
Where giggles and silliness roam wild and free.

Tides of Light in Motion

Marbles of sunshine spill on the floor,
A cat wearing glasses, ready to roar.
Jellybean surfers ride on the waves,
Making grand plans to build jelly caves.

Dancing on shadows, the cupcakes unite,
Debating the merits of sprinkles—what's right?
While giggly clouds play a game of charades,
A worm serenades from under some blades.

Flip-flop fish splash with a splashy cheer,
While a toad jumps up, proclaiming he's here!
Laughing at daisies who dance out of sync,
They're out of control—oh, what will they think?

With light on our faces, we skip down the lane,
Joining this circus of joy and of pain.
Tides of laughter roll, bounce off the trees,
In this riotous whirl, we do as we please!

A Haven of Golden Tranquility

In a world of winks, where giggles reside,
Lemonade fountains, all joy and pride.
Bicycles chatter, their wheels in a spin,
While puddles reflect all the mayhem within.

Time turns to rubber, a stretchy delight,
With frogs hosting parties, oh what a sight!
A pie-baking contest, a race with a fox,
They're sprouting tall tales from baker's paradox.

Pineapples wear hats, sipping on tea,
As the ants in tuxedos just watch and agree.
Butterflies gossip, their wings all aglow,
Painting this haven with vibrant flow.

Where silliness reigns in bright sunlight's wink,
And laughter's the currency, more fun than you think.
Let's dance with the shadows and twirl with the breeze,
In this golden tranquility, we do as we please!

Breathless Moments Under Brilliance

Chasing after rainbows, with shoes made of air,
A cat in a bowtie, flips through its glare.
Jousting with lizards, they brandish their tails,
While balancing cake on magnificent rails.

With stars in our pockets, we jump into dreams,
Rearranging the world, or so it seems.
Bubble-blowing turtles swim happily round,
While moonbeams nod off, not making a sound.

Squirrels tell stories of nuts they once lost,
Weighty opinions come at quite a cost.
A parrot in slippers performs with great flair,
In a dance-off with shadows, do we dare?

Giggling gumdrops slide down a hill,
As we seize breathless moments, oh what a thrill!
Here under brilliance, we'll laugh 'til we drop,
In the joyful chaos, we never will stop.

Flashes of Warmth Beneath the Canopy

Beneath the leafy cover, squirrels dance in line,
A robin sings a tune, it's such a sweet design.
The ant parade is marching, they've got a funny flair,
While I'm just here, pretending I have no care.

A breeze fluffs up my hair, my hat's gone on a trip,
The sun peeks through the branches, gives my nose a flip.

I chase after my cap with all the grace of clay,
Rolling like a tumbleweed, what a silly play!

My picnic's all laid out, but where's my sandwich gone?
The raccoons plot and scheme, they've sprung a lunchtime con.
With crumbs flying high as kites, they raid my tasty stash,

I laugh and shake my fist, wish I could make a dash.

So here I sit and chuckle, at nature's grand charade,
A stage of silly moments, in sunlight's glowing shade.
It's fun to lose my stuff, in such a vibrant scene,
Where laughter is a treasure, though the ants are quite a glean.

Soft Hues of Morning Embrace

The dawn arrives like laughter, tickling sleepy skies,
While coffee's brewing slowly, we catch the sunrise flies.

In pajama fashion statements, we glide across the floor,
With mismatched socks and giggles, who could ask for more?

The toast jumps out like popcorn, a dance that makes us grin,
We've got a cat that serenades, with purring from within.
As curtains sway like dancers, with sunlight's crazy sway,

We join the morning madness, to chase our woes away.

The baby plants are wiggling, trying hard to grow,
While I'm tripping over shoes, that's how my mornings go.
Yet every tiny laughter, lights the day anew,
With soft and silly moments, that makes the world a hue.

So here's to all the mischief, the coffee stains and cheer,
In every little chaos, we find what we hold dear.
The mornings filled with sunshine, are never quite the same,
When laughter's the companion, that ignites the playful flame.

The Haven of Illuminated Solitude

Oh, the chair I've claimed as mine, it creaks beneath my weight,
With sunlight sneaking in through cracks, it's quite a funny fate.
A book lies open on my lap, I've read the same page twice,
Yet here I sit, enthralled by where the quiet feels so nice.

The dust motes dance like fairies, they swirl and giggle here,
While outside there's a racket, the world spins full of cheer.
I find this being lazy stuff, my comfy little nook,
Has laughing echoes from the past, like pages from a book.

The neighbor's cat now peeks in, with curious round eyes,

We stare in silent contest, oh what a grand surprise!
I hold my breath, it holds its tail, it's like a royal show,
A showdown in the warmth of light, where only we can glow.

So let the world be noisy, with its hustle and its jive,
I'll stay here in my sunshine, where funny thoughts arrive.

For solitude is joyous, when laughter's in the air,
A hidden spot of brilliance, and I am happy there.

Finding Peace Within the Glow

A lamp that flickers softly, casts shadows on the wall,
With goofy shapes and stories, I giggle through it all.
The glow invites sweet chaos, my mind begins to race,
As I invent a monster, that wears a silly face.

The clock ticks in the corner, with a rhythm like a tune,
While outside it's raining cats, and dogs are dancing soon.

I hear their wriggly giggles, beneath the cover quick,
I'm safe within my cozy glow, where humor does the trick.

My teacup has a secret, it whispers when I sip,
It tells me wild adventures, like living on a ship.
With every little chuckle, my fears begin to flee,
As laughter sparkles in the light, it's just my cup and me.

So let the world get wild out there, with every twist and turn,
I'll stay right here and chuckle, as the lanterns softly burn.

For peace is found in goofiness, within a glowing space,
Where joy ignites the shadows, and shines upon my face.

Timeless Gleams in Hidden Corners

In a nook where shadows play,
A cat can sunbathe all day.
He dreams of fish, so grand and bright,
While birds just laugh, what a sight!

A sock that hides, and dust bunnies,
Chasing each other, how funny!
They dance their waltz, no care in view,
While I just sneeze, oh joy, ado!

A spot so cozy, yet unclear,
Where laughter blooms from every cheer.
My tea spills down, not on the floor,
'Twas a great leap—now there's much more!

By the window's edge, I sit amazed,
At how such small things leave me crazed.
Moments of glee in each little beam,
Life's silly tricks, oh sweet daydream!

Enchanted by the Glare of Serenity

The sunbeams bounce like kids at play,
While squirrels plot their nutty way.
They giggle as they race and hide,
In the enchanted woods, they collide!

A butterfly with a flair for dance,
Whirls and twirls, it's quite a chance.
It lands on my nose, what a surprise,
Together we laugh, oh how time flies!

The flowers nod with a cheeky grin,
As I trip and fall, then hop right in.
Their petals whisper sweet, silly things,
Even the grass has its own swing!

From sunlit heights, to shadows so sly,
Nature's my stage, oh my, oh my!
With every step, I join the mirth,
In this odd little world, I find my worth!

Where Light and Nature Coalesce

Light filters through with a sneaky laugh,
As I mistakenly take the wrong path.
A leaf lands gently on my head,
It seems to say, "Let's go instead!"

The fish in the pond wear hats of glee,
While frogs croak out a symphony.
A tiny bird plays peek-a-boo,
I wave and say, "I see you too!"

Dandelions puff with silly pride,
While bees zoom past for a wild ride.
They buzz, and dance, like they know the score,
I can't help but chuckle, always wanting more!

Nature's making fun, it's not so serious,
Yet I can't stop giggling, it's so delirious.
With every bright ray and critter's tease,
Life's little jests bring me to my knees!

Vibrant Reflections on Gentle Waters

Ripples laugh at ducks on parade,
While I sit back, my plans now delayed.
With each splash, my snack takes flight,
I didn't think ducks could be such a fright!

In the mirror of water, oh what a sight,
My silly face, it gives me a fright.
Fish below giggle, it's their grand show,
As I wave back with my chipmunk glow!

Dragonflies zoom, they look so dapper,
While I'm flailing, hoping for a clapper.
They toast to my clumsiness, what a charade,
In this bustling world, my debts are repaid!

As the day wanes and the laughs don't cease,
Every splash and chuckle brings me peace.
For wherever water flows and twinkles so bright,
Laughter's the treasure that feels just right!

The Flourish of Bright Moments

In the garden where the daisies dance,
Squirrels plot a sneaky prance.
A butterfly gave a cheeky wink,
While the neighbor's dog began to stink.

Laughter bubbles like a springing brook,
As kids play hooky from every book.
With lemonade stained smiles so wide,
Even the ants have joined this ride.

Pigeons strut in a goofy parade,
Chasing crumbs like a hungry brigade.
Oh, the joy in each little fling,
Who knew that veggies could make us sing?

These light moments sing with zest,
In life's playful and silly fest.
With each giggle, a memory is spun,
A bouquet of fun, a day well done.

Blessings of the Daylight

The rooster crows, a noisy guide,
Chasing away the blanket of night.
Coffee spills as we rush and race,
Who knew mornings could wear such a face?

Birds get tangled in a song so wild,
They chirp and squawk, a raucous child.
Meanwhile, socks lose their pair by fate,
As we laugh at the strange state of late.

Sunbeams tickle the tips of our toes,
While the cat takes an ungraceful doze.
Even the goldfish looks a tad mad,
Swimming in circles like a confused lad.

Giggling under the warm embrace,
We bless these silly moments of grace.
With daylight comes shenanigans bright,
As chaos reigns until the night.

A Whiff of Nature's Brilliance

A daisy sneezed amid a breeze,
While veggies chuckled, "Oh please!"
Grasshoppers hopped as if on cue,
Bouncing with glee, they joined the crew.

Oh, the flowers in their vibrant dress,
Places to hide if you want to jest.
Bees buzzing loud, not quiet at all,
Claiming their space in the garden's hall.

The wind whispers secrets to the trees,
Who giggle softly as they tease.
Squirrels toss acorns like tiny bombs,
While we lose patience for nature's qualms.

Frogs in ponds croak a funny tune,
Joking around beneath the moon.
Every blossom springs a smile today,
In this wacky nature ballet.

Radiating Joy in Color

From red to blue, the colors shout,
A parade of hues, a joyful clout.
Crayons scribble thoughts anew,
In a funky hue, they start to skew.

With oranges jiving, yellows strut,
At the paint party, no room for a rut.
Green swirls giggle, "We're feeling bold!"
While purple pirouettes, oh so uncontrolled.

The canvas dances like it's alive,
Each smudge promising a silly dive.
Rainbows pop in a colorful spree,
Giggling along with the buzzing bee.

We paint our joy, let laughter glow,
In the art of fun, we steal the show.
With every brushstroke, a memory made,
In vibrant tones, this escapade!

When Daylight Dances

The cat leaps high, it thinks it's a star,
Yet lands in a pot, how bizarre!
Light spills laughter in corners wide,
As it tickles the toes of a giggling child.

Flowers gossip with buzzing bees,
While squirrels play tag with the softest breeze.
A rabbit hops, then takes a bow,
Oh, the fun that daylight endows!

Chasing shadows, we spin around,
In this theater where joy is found.
The sun grins down from its lofty throne,
Inviting us all to dance alone.

With every twirl, we lose our cares,
In sunbeam flickers, we find our fares.
Yet somehow, I still trip and fall,
Laughter erupts, and we answer the call.

Warmth Between the Leaves

A ticklish breeze ruffles my hair,
As I spot a chipmunk stealing my fare.
He thinks he's sly among the trees,
But I'm just here for the afternoon tease.

The sunlight peeks through branches wide,
Highlighting what the creatures hide.
A worm wears sunglasses, oh what a sight,
While leaves gossip and giggle with light.

I take a sip of my berry juice,
And a gang of ants march, what's their excuse?
The warm air hums a cheerful tune,
As dandelions plot to rise up soon.

So with a blanket and snacks galore,
I join this party—oh, who could ask for more?
In this leafy haven, we linger and play,
Where silliness reigns the livelong day.

Beams of Serenity

With beams of light, there's a merry mishap,
A raccoon crashes through, wearing a cap.
He steals the picnic, such cunning finesse,
While squirrels cheer on, "He's the best in this mess!"

The daisies sway, poking fun at me,
As I trip on roots, oh how can this be?
The butterflies snicker, flitting away,
As I practice my dance, just trying to play.

A noodle of sunlight wraps 'round my shoe,
While grass tickles toes—it's a silly view.
We laugh with the breeze, a merry old crew,
In patches of warmth, where fun just grew.

The day drips down like melting ice cream,
With laughter and antics that always redeem.
As the sun dips low, we all wave goodbye,
To the beams of serenity shining in the sky.

Light's Embrace on Morning Dew

Morning breaks with a wink and a nod,
As I slip on grass that feels quite odd.
A frog croaks loudly, claiming the stage,
While the dew drops giggle, releasing their rage.

The flowers yawn, stretching their petals wide,
While I watch a snail take a slippery ride.
With each tiny squish, there's a hilarious cheer,
As morning embraces us all, oh dear!

A ladybug dances around on my nose,
I sneeze and it twirls, oh where all it goes!
The sun's soft tickle makes shadows play,
In this whimsical world, we dance and sway.

So here's to the morning, with laughter and glee,
Where every odd moment holds clarity.
With light's embrace and joy in view,
Let's take on each day with a smile anew!

Interludes of Joy in Shimmering Spaces

In a meadow of giggles, the flowers dance,
Butterflies in sunglasses take a chance.
Bees hold a picnic, sipping on nectar,
While ants in tuxedos serve insect projector.

A squirrel on a trampoline does a flip,
Chasing after acorns, he's lost his grip.
With a squeaky laugh, he lands on a clover,
While ladybugs cheer him on, ever sober.

Laughter echoes through the trees, so bright,
As frogs wear bowties for the fancy night.
Each joke like confetti, floats through the air,
In this wacky world, joy's everywhere!

So if you feel gray, come join the parade,
In these shimmering realms, the fun won't fade.
Let giggles and grins light up your face,
For every heart deserves a warm embrace.

Glowing Trails of Daydreams

A cat in a top hat, with a cane so neat,
Struts down the path, he's a real cool treat.
The clouds wear pajamas, drifting so slow,
While stars play hopscotch in evening's glow.

Dancing in sunlight, a merry-go-round,
Makes lettuce hats for bunnies all around.
With each leap and bound, they giggle so loud,
As beetles breakdance, beneath the cloud.

In the corner, a snail's on a skateboard,
Zipping past daisies, it's quite the reward.
With a wink and a smile, he passes the time,
In this world of whimsy, all is sublime.

As daydreams spin round like a carnival ride,
Join in the laughter, let worries subside.
In these glowing trails, where fun is the fate,
Savor the moments, it's never too late.

Shadows Play Beneath Golden Horizons

Here in the twilight, shadows wear shoes,
Playing tag with the light, unfazed by the blues.
They leap like dancers, swirling so free,
While crickets compose a sweet symphony.

A dog on a pogo stick hops to the beat,
Chasing after his tail in a flash of heat.
While shadows cascade in a cheerful embrace,
They tumble and twirl, in a playful race.

As the sun dips down, it spills golden cheer,
And whispers sweet nothings for all, far and near.
With giggling leaves swirling in dizzy delight,
Shadows descend, throwing a wild light.

So sway with the laughter, let your heart play,
In the dance of the evening, all worries can sway.
For in these shadowed realms, where dreams do ignite,
Find the humor in life, and let it take flight.

The Kiss of Daybreak on Gentle Petals

As daybreak tiptoes, the flowers blink wide,
Dewdrops giggle, as if they're a guide.
The daisies wear crowns, looking quite grand,
While dandelions plot a wildflower band.

The tulips are gossiping, leaning in tight,
Discussing the antics of stars in the night.
The sun's playful poke gets them all in a whirl,
And butterflies flit, making their hearts twirl.

With patter of petals, the bees start to hum,
While frogs in top hats sing the morning's drum.
Every chirp and giggle brings joy to the morn,
In this quirky garden, creativity's born.

So whenever the dawn brings a new kind of glow,
Just dance with the flowers, let your laughter flow.
For moments so silly, we cherish with friends,
In nature's warm laughter, the joy never ends.

www.ingramcontent.com/pod-product-compliance
Lightning Source LLC
Chambersburg PA
CBHW070312120526
44590CB00017B/2643